THINGS TO PRAY FOR

BY

S. GAINES

Table of Contents

Prologue

It once was an old lady that prayed everyday faithfully for 20 years that she would win the lottery one day to be able to help her kids and grandchildren before her time up on earth. She prayed that prayer faithfully until the day she left this earth and went to heaven. As she walked around enjoying her new life she decided she would ask the lord why out of all the things she prayed for the lord never answered that one. So she goes to one of the Angels and say hey I would like to speak to the lord and he says ok no problem but first is it anything that maybe I can help you with and she say yes I would like to ask how come out of all the prayers I've sent up here how come i never received the one about winning the lottery. The angel looks at her smile and says out of all your prayers you've sent us that's the one we've answered the most but you see in order for you to win the lottery you have to buy a ticket first.

Chapter 1:
Introduction to Praise

We all pray to someone for blessings, protections, guidance and a variety of things we feel and believe are out of our hands. But in reality we may just be praying wrong. One of the biggest mistakes I've made through my life of praying is once I use to pray, I'll put it in God's hand and then go about my day waiting for my blessing to come. I learned the hard way by sending up your prayers, having faith in them and then getting up, kicking down doors and going out to make those blessings come to life offered me 10x more results. The 1st stage in learning how to pray is to first identify what kind of prayer you are. I say that the concept of your style of praying is as essential to you as your fingerprints. I will break down the different types of prayers I've come across in my research and suggest to each about how to get away from them and onto the path of the one you wish to be. This book isn't based on one religion. It doesn't matter who you pray to. I have no control over anyone's faith. I'm just a vessel delivering a message. It's about teaching you to pray to them the correct way.

"Purpose can add not only years to your life but life

to your years as well"

-Richard Leider

Chapter 2:
The Imperfection Prayer

Some people don't pray correctly because they feel like they are not good enough to receive the blessing they wish to ask for because they fluent between sinning their everyday life and the path of righteousness they wish to be on they will put the praise to the side with the idea when they get better they will put more effort into it I was once this kind of prayer and to me this onesies the most incompetent of them all because we are the most lost of the sheep and need the most guidance of them all so by accepting our sin and praying for forgiveness is the only way to find grace to move forward to the path of righteousness. By accepting this fully without holding back you should feel a vibe of positive energy sweep through you. This energy is the Holy Spirit and if you speak what you mean from your heart and not your mind then I promise you will see the results of your prayers.

"Good is the enemy of great"

-Jim Collins

Chapter 3:

A Worrying Prayer

This may be the biggest type of prayer out of them all, because it almost seems to be human nature to worry about everything that we have no control over. I think the reason for that is because of fear. We are afraid that the worst outcome will come out of a situation that may not even take place. In order to come to the concept of having faith in your prayer we must first understand the boundaries of one praying. See prayer will change things but it will not pay off our debts to karma so if we are in a situation from a seed we planted then we will reap what we sow. So you must not pray to get out of the situation you must divert your prayer to give you guidance to understand how you shall overcome this situation you must have a clear mind to ask for strength to stand through the outcome of your situation .See praying is not a do over card it is more of a help and tutorial tab. Instead of asking for an outcome to your situation, ask for comfort to accept whatever may come out of your situation.

"Fate is shaped half by expectation and half by inattention"

-Amy Tan The Joy Luck Club

Chapter 4:

A Lost Prayer

I remember some dark times in my life where I didn't have anyone to turn to, my back was against the wall and I knew I had to pray but I had no idea how. I know I prayed so many times in so many different ways but yet I had no idea if it was the correct way or the reason why because my mind was lost. I was so stuck in my problems and pain I didn't understand what I was doing. I notice now that I was just having a conversation with God instead of praying to him and that is a difference in itself. I realized that if I cleared my mind and empty my heart into them, the same conversation words flowed from me naturally asking for things you didn't know I wanted and during those types of conversations is when I can feel the chills run through my body. So don't just have a conversation with the lord, pray to him and if you don't feel the shivers run through you before you say Amen then you're not praying right.

Do not go where the path may lead, go instead where there is no path and leave a trail.

-Ralph Waldo Emerson

Chapter 5:
Meditation Praying

A meditating prayer is on the right track to praying fully, they isolate themselves from their surroundings and focus on the direct connection between them and the lord. Their mind is clear and free from all worrying and pain. They are locally at peace within themselves at the moment which in itself is the complete problem with their praying. Putting yourself at peace before you pray is muting out your heart from sending the soul pain through your spirit to deliver the message of the healing your desire from the Lord .Your mind is the vessel that holds all the knowledge you gain. But to me your heart is the closest thing to your soul and if nothing else does your heart will know right and wrong so follow it during your prayer, listen to it ,feel it and it will not leave you astray.

"Faith is acceptance of which we imagine to be true, that we cannot prove."

-Dan Brown The Da Vinci Code

Chapter 6:

Things To Pray For

I t's crazy how a man with as many issues as me, a person who is so confused, lost and unbalanced in life is getting this calling to write this book about praying. The words flow through me as they pour out into what you are reading now. I'm now some perfect person in life that got everything together on the right track. In reality I'm the complete opposite. My life is upside down and I've just come out of a miserable point where I couldn't get anything to do right. People were betraying me, people were dying around me and my enemies were dancing in triumph of my defeat. I was losing faith until tonight I dropped down to my knees and prayed to the lord like my life depended on it. We must learn that praying isn't the key to blessing, it's what to pray for that can make a difference. The next couple of chapters I will break down 25 things to pray for that will make a difference that you didn't even know you needed.

"Aerodynamically the bumblebee shouldn't be able to fly, but the bumblebee doesn't know that it so goes on flying anyway"

-Mary Kay Ash

Chapter 7:

A Clear Path

A clear path from your enemies, That he guides you from all those that plan against you. Just the simple prayer of the clear path will give you so many different results. It will overshadow you with protection from negative spirits/energies. It will stop those plotting harm against you, it will give you a better vision to make decisions or stressful situations that you will run across. Add the prayer for a clear path from your enemies and you will notice your journey becoming noticeably a little easier.

"If you don't know where you going, any road will get you there"

-Lewis Carroll

Chapter 8:

A long happy and successful life

Instead of targeting certain goals to just happen at a specific time. Try praying for success in longevity and have faith in letting things play out for the better, To me praying for a long, happy, and successful life is like saying Lord I have faith in you to reward me for my righteousness, that you might not come as I wish but when you feel as I'm ready. This prayer is giving the lord a bigger window of opportunity to deliver his blessing to you at any point in your life, it's asking for him to deliver you health, to accomplish your goals and to find happiness in different aspects of your life. This prayer is so powerful because it's not you telling the lord what you need help with its asking him to look at your life and fix everything he sees wrong with it, its asking him to grab your wrist and lead you to paths you cannot see to reach happiness, its asking him to give you vision and understanding to make decision that you do not understand to reach your destiny yes to me this is a prayer not only you should pray for yourself but for your family and loved ones as well.

"As you think so shall you become"

-Bruce Lee

Chapter 9:

Freedom

Everyone should have the desire to never stop growing and learning. That is freedom to be able to go beyond your limits at will. To have that push in you to keep going until you accomplish the impossible. We all have witnessed regular people accomplish great things that make us question the difference between them and us. This is the freedom within them they choose whether to give up or not and that is what elevates them to the next level. The prayer for freedom is a great way to achieve success in your physical, mental, spiritual, financial, and social area of your life. There's so much to learn and see in life and unless you learn to kick down the doors of our boundaries we will remain confined. Your destiny is in your own hand and praying for freedom will allow you to dictate the outcome of it.

"If you want to make your dreams come true, the first thing you have to do is wake up."

-J.M. Power

Chapter 10:
Been Thankful For The Tiny Moments

We all are so busy living and working that we don't have time to give the lord a full prayer. We try to say a quick prayer and highlight the important part as if that is good enough. One of the most important things about praying is to also give thanks for the small things we have. This might not seem as important but in reality it really is because the things you overlook are things that someone else prays for. Simple tiny moments that we enjoy but over look like finding change or a dollar in a pair of your old jeans. Watching your favorite tv show when you're sick and being comforted by a loved one, or seeing a cashier opens up a new checkout lane and she waves you over. Now imagine you've been hungry on the corner asking for change, imagine you've been homesick and your mom working overnight to provide for you. Those tiny moments I'm so thankful for can easily be the big moments I pray for. Don't just pray and ask and give thanks as well learn to pray with them both will make you an example of a complete prayer.

"The smallest good deed is better than the greatest

good intention"

-Joseph Duquet

Chapter 11:

Forgiveness

Praying for forgiveness is a touchy subject for me because I'm not just asking for forgiveness for my sins I'm asking for forgiveness for everything I've ever done wrong. People I've crossed disappointed, embarrassed, lied to or caused physical or mental abuse to. Getting forgiveness is a major step in life. It will free you of your burdens and take weight off of your heart.

"Much unhappiness comes into the world because of bewilderment and things left unsaid"

-Fyodor Dostoyevsky

Chapter 12:

Angels To Watch Over Me

This may seem weird and awkward but I found comfort in praying for my loved ones that have died and gone on to the next life. I Prayed that they found their way into heaven and that they would look over me every now and then to keep me safe and guide me. I pray that they find peace.

It is during our darkest moments that we must focus to see the light.

-Aristotle

Chapter 13:
Strength

The reason why praying for strength is so important to me is because your praying grows as the person whose praying grows. The praying will strengthen as the prayer strengthens. The more powerful the person that is praying , the more powerful the prayer will be. The concept of this chapter is if you become stronger as a whole, you will become strong mentally, physically, and spiritually. Which allows you to uplift your burden as if the lord lightens them. With the prayer of strength you will become a rock of positive energy that will bring stability to those around you. Having strength in you can make unexpected changes around and in people that you didn't even imagine would have a butterfly effect for your strength alone.

"Darkness cannot drive out darkness, Only light can do that Hate cannot drive out hate, Only love can do that "

-Martin Luther King Jr.

Chapter 14:

A testimony of peace.

A testimony of peace of prayer. It is so full of excitement seeing the things we prayed for come to life. given the things and comforts we longed for to the dreams of our desire. At this moment this is when you can lose everything by gaining it all. let me say that again you can lose everything by gaining it all and i say that to say this. people become the most stagnant and complacent during their time of peace so at this point you will start praying less, understanding less, seeing less again because that hole in your soul has been filled. you no longer feel that draw of power pulling you because at this point mentally you suppose to be there.i'm a strong believer in everything happens for a reason but i also believe your decisions in life dictates what are some of the things that do happen.

You must be the change you wish to see in the world.

-Mahatma Gandhi

Chapter 15:
Peace and protection

This chapter is for them days, nights, moments when something is off but everything is what it should be as if you can feel it. As if you can sense it those are the storms that brewing. It's the quiet before the storm to come, the best way to defeat the unseen or known is to prepare for it. To ask that peace and protection remains around you at all times for the things that seen and unseen it's so much going on in the existing of your life it can be overwhelming to just think of all the things that can go wrong in life. Let your praying adapt to your life until it take on the identity of who you are. You have a heart. A soul. A mind. Joy pain and understanding use them to become a prayer of you instead of seeking powers from words that were written with no vibrational ties to them. I made so many mistakes in life I can't begin to explain how I got to writing a book of this nature but I'm happy of my journey and who I've become. I remember nights with a home but nowhere to go so I just sat in my car and listened to music, closing my eyes and just escaping. I don't know where I use to go or what I use toner away from but it help me. I turned my conversations with the most high into my prayers. Instead of asking and demanding I told him of my pain and suffering my doubts and fears my joy and pain and eventually things started changing for me doors started to open more and weight was lifted from upon my shoulders.

The future belongs to those who believe in the beauty of their dreams.

-Eleanor Roosevelt

Epilogue

ooking back on life and the things I've been through and survived, I came to grasp that regardless of how many self help books you read, advice you've given, directions you've pointed. no one can find your way in life but you. No one has to live your life but you and you're the only that can live it. so don't get caught up in looking for all the answers concerning your life in others when no one else has lived it before you. I hope some of the things that were said in this book were of use to someone out there and that the words hold values to help them get out of whatever it may be that they're going through in life. I've overcome a lot of my trials and tribulations and life but as I continue to live a new day upon this earth I gladly accept and understand that I will face new challenges and weather new storms in the paths ahead of me. With that said I will bring this book to an end and wish you all the best and my love, peace and protection find you with your many years on this earth.

9 789696 479230